Robert B. Brough

Songs of the Governing Classes

Robert B. Brough

Songs of the Governing Classes

ISBN/EAN: 9783337130626

Printed in Europe, USA, Canada, Australia, Japan

Cover: Foto ©Thomas Meinert / pixelio.de

More available books at **www.hansebooks.com**

SONGS

OF THE

"GOVERNING CLASSES,"

AND OTHER LYRICS.

WRITTEN IN A SEASONABLE SPIRIT OF "VULGAR DECLAMATION."

BY ROBERT B. BROUGH.

NEW EDITION.

LONDON:

VIZETELLY & CO., 16 HENRIETTA STREET,
COVENT GARDEN.
1890.

J. MILLER AND SON, PRINTERS, EDINBURGH

"The gentlemen who just about this time (1855)
were establishing a new school of critical literature
were constantly either savagely ferocious or bitterly
sarcastic with professional literary men—persons,
that is to say, who lived by the product of their
pens, who in most cases had not had the advantage
of that university education in which their de-
tractors gloried, and which enabled them to turn
the Ode to Thaliarchus into halting English verse,
or to imbue with a few classical allusions their
fierce political essay or flippant critical review.
And, save that he was endowed with more and
finer brains than the average run of humanity,
Robert Brough was the exact type of the class
thus bitterly reviled. Spurning the life of com-
mercial drudgery to which he was orginally des-
tined, he commenced on his own account at a very
early age, and awoke the echoes of his dull prosaic
town with the cracking of his witty whip. The

Liverpool Lion was a new feature in the annals of the Mersey's pride.

"Those who wish to inform themselves of the manner of Robert Brough's early life-work should read his novel 'Marston Lynch,' of which the author is the hero. I say early life-work; but it was all, in fact, early enough, for he was but five or six and thirty when he died. But in the *Liverpool Lion* is to be seen the germ of most of what distinguished his later writings—the bright wit, the strange quaint fancy, the readiness to seize upon topics of the hour, and present them in the quaintest garb: the exquisite pathos was not there, nor the bitter savagery, though gleams of this last were not wanting.

"I have often wondered what gave Robert Brough that deep vindictive hatred of wealth and rank and respectability which permeated his life. It was probably innate; it was certainly engrained. It was largely increased by poverty, by ill health, by an ill-regulated life, by an ever present conviction that there lay in him power to produce work of very superior quality to that already published— power which was nullified by his own weakness of will. His was the poetic temperament, sensitive, nervous, irritable; his too the craving after ignoble sources of alleviation in times of mental depression, and the impossibility of resisting temptation, come in what form it might.*

"He was a Radical, a Republican even, but something—partly his gentle nature, and doubtless greatly his wonderfully keen perception of the ludicrous—kept him from emulating the literary achievements of the political contributors to the cheap Sunday press. His was not the coarse many-syllabled fustian of a 'Publicola' or a 'Gracchus,' produced according to the laws of demand and supply, and paid for by a weekly wage. Robert Brough's was the real fierce hatred welling up from an embittered soul, and finding its vent in verse. Here is the *mot de l'enigme* :

" ' There is a word in the English tongue,
    Where I'd rather it were not ;
For shame and lies from it have sprung,
    And heart burns fierce and hot :
'Tis a tawdry cloak for a dirty soul :
    'Tis a sanctuary base,
Where the fool and the knave themselves may save
    From justice and disgrace :
'Tis a curse to the land, deny it who can,
    That self-same boast, 'I'm a gentleman.'

* "On his twenty-ninth birthday he wrote me a letter commencing :
        " 'I'm twenty-nine ! I'm twenty-nine !
        I've drank too much of beer and wine ;
        I've had too much of love and strife ;
        I've given a kiss to Johnson's wife,
        And sent a lying note to mine—
        I'm twenty-nine ! I'm twenty-nine !'

"That is the opening of a poem contained in a little thin volume called 'Songs of the Governing Classes,' by Robert Brough, published in 1855, the year of which I am writing, by Vizetelly. It had scarcely any sale, and has been unprocurable for many years. From the freedom of its speech, the vigour of its thought, and the polish of its workmanship, it was a very remarkable production."

PREFACE TO THE FIRST EDITION.

I HAVE been advised not to print my name to this volume of poems, (for poems I believe they are to be called, if bad ones) on the grounds, that being only known (where at all) as a "profane jester and satirist,"* the public will refuse to take me *au serieux;* and that what is at all events an attempted expression of earnest convictions, will stand a risk of being passed by as a collection of ephemeral squibs written in a spirit of the merest tomfoolery

* Mr Ruskin, of Salvator Rosa.

Admitting the business-like force of the argument, I confess the proposed conditions appear rather too humiliating for compliance with. Seeing no reason to feel ashamed of my offspring, I cannot be brought to admit that my offspring should, as it were, blush for their parent. I have certainly made jokes for a livelihood, just as I should have made boots, if I had been brought up to the business (believing that there is no harm or disgrace in either calling, so long as nobody's corns are unfairly pinched); but I do not see that I am thereby disqualified from giving serious utterance to my feelings on vital questions, affecting me as well as my neighbours. The honest mountebank, with his paint washed off and seedy surtout buttoned over his spangles—reduced, in fact, to the level of a mere anxious-faced taxpayer—has surely as much right to raise his voice at a public meeting as his fellow-sufferer the shoemaker. Nay, if long practice in "the ring" have given him a greater command of the powers of sarcasm, ridicule, and inuendo, than his brethren in the gallery, should he not be rather encouraged to a hearing ?

The feeling of which the following ballads are the faint echo and imperfect expression, is a deeply-rooted belief that to the institution of aristocracy in this country (not merely to its "undue preponderance," but to its absolute existence) is mainly attributable all the political injustice, and more especially the grovelling moral debasement, we have to deplore— a feeling by no means recently implanted or even greatly developed in the writer's heart, but one which the preparation of the public mind by recent events and disclosures* has afforded him the opportunity of spreading

* This had reference to the War in the Crimea.

to the best of his ability, and by such means of utterance as he had at his disposal.

June 28, 1855.

DEDICATION

PREFIXED TO THE FIRST EDITION.

TO EDWARD M. WHITTY,

AUTHOR OF "THE GOVERNING CLASSES OF GREAT
BRITAIN."

My Dear Whitty,

Accept the dedication of a volume, which, if not
indebted to you for immediate suggestion, certainly
owes to your inimitable *exposé* of the Fundamental
Wrong of this Country, much of that awakened
public feeling which alone could have rendered its
publication possible.

I believe in the Revolution you have said is com-
ing—however slowly—and with precocious eager-
ness seize this opportunity of tacking my name on
to the skirts of one, that will be reverenced (I

think I see your astonishment!) by future reapers in the open field, as that of one of the first and bravest pioneers to bring an axe into the forest.

My modest song book, to your terrible story book, aspires to be no more than the fiddle that plays while the majestic panorama is unrolling; still, if the fiddle plays well, it may contribute its share to the general popularity of "the entertainment." Should a single one of my tunes arrive at the dignity of being whistled in the street, I shall grudge neither resin nor elbow.

Your old friend, and sincere admirer,

ROBERT B. BROUGH.

CONTENTS.

PORTRAITS.

		PAGE
I.—THE MARQUIS OF CARABAS	. . .	19
II.—MY LORD TOMNODDY	. . .	24
III.—THE EARL OF WHITECHOKERLEA	. .	27
IV.—LORD CHARLES CLEVERLEY	. . .	31
V.—SIR MENENIUS AGRIPPA, THE FRIEND OF THE		
PEOPLE		35
VI.—SIR GYPES TOLLODDLE		39

HISTORIC FANCIES.

THE RETURN FROM SYRIA	. . . .	47
THE INCAS OF PERU	. . . . .	52
THE APOLOGUE OF CORIOLANUS	. . .	58
A WORD FOR NERO	. . . : .	67
GODIVA .	. . . . . .	72
"WANTED, AN INDIVIDUAL" .	. . .	80

MISCELLANIES.

	PAGE
"Vulgar Declamation"	87
The Terriers, the Rats, the Mice, and the Cats— A Fable	90
Who's Afraid?—A Taunt	100
Ca Ira. A Song for Ministers . . .	105
The Strawberry Leaf	109
"A Gentleman"	111
French and English—A Morality from the Trenches	114
A Few Questions	118
A Few More	119

PORTRAITS.

B

I.—THE MARQUIS OF CARABAS.

A SONG WITH A STOLEN BURDEN.*

OFF with your hat! along the streets

His Lordship's carriage rolls;

Respect to greatness—when it shines

To cheer our darken'd souls.

Get off the step, you ragged boys!

Policeman, where's your staff?

This is a sight to check with awe

The most irrev'rent laugh.

Chapeau bas!

Chapeau bas!

Gloire au Marquis de Carabas!

* The *refrain* of one of Beranger's most popular and in every sense of the word) stirring lyrics of the Restoration. Beyond this the two songs have nothing in common, with the possible exception of sincerity.

Stand further back ! we'll see him well ;
　　Wait till they lift him out :
It takes some time ; his Lordship's old,
　　And suffers from the gout.
Now look ! he owns a castled park
　　For ev'ry finger thin ;
He has more sterling pounds a-day
　　Than wrinkles on his skin.
　　　　　Chapeau bas !
　　　　　Chapeau bas !
　　　Gloire au Marquis de Carabas !

The founder of his race was son
　　To a king's cousin, rich ;
(The mother was an oyster wench—
　　She perish'd in a ditch).
His patriot worth, embalm'd has been
　　In poet's loud applause :
He made twelve thousand pounds a-year
　　By aiding France's cause.
　　　　　Chapeau bas !
　　　　　Chapeau bas !
　　　Gloire au Marquis de Carabas !

The second marquis, of the stole
Was groom to th' second James;
He all but caught that recreant king
When flying o'er the Thames.
Devotion rare! by Orange Will
With a Scotch county paid;
He gain'd one more—in Ireland—when
Charles Edward he betray'd.
Chapeau bas!
Chapeau bas!
Gloire au Marquis de Carabas!

He liv'd to see his son grow up
A gen'ral famed and bold,
Who fought his country's fights—and *one*
For half a million, sold.
His son (alas! the house's shame)
Fritter'd the name away:
Diced, wench'd, and drank—at last got shot,
Through cheating in his play!
Chapeau bas!
Chapeau bas!
Gloire au Marquis de Carabas!

Now, see, where, focus'd on one head,
  The race's glories shine :
The head gets narrow at the top,
  But mark the jaw—how fine !
Don't call it satyr-like ; you'd wound
  Some scores, whose honest pates,
The selfsame type present, upon
  The Carabas estates !
      Chapeau bas !
      Chapeau bas !
    Gloire au Marquis de Carabas !

Look at his skin—at four-score years
  How fresh it gleams, and fair :
He never tasted ill-dress'd food,
  Or breath'd in tainted air.
The noble blood glows through his viens
  Still, with a healthful pink ;
His brow scarce wrinkled !—Brows keep so
  That have not got to think.
      Chapeau bas !
      Chapeau bas !
    Gloire au Marquis de Carabas !

His hand's unglove'd !—it shakes, 'tis true
  But mark its tiny size,
(High birth's true sign) and shape, as on
  The lackey's arm it lies.
That hand ne'er penn'd a useful line,
  Ne'er work'd a deed of fame
Save slaying one, whose sister he—
  Its owner—brought to shame.
     Chapeau bas!
     Chapeau bas!
  Gloire au Marquis de Carabas!

They've got him in—he's gone to vote
  Your rights and mine away ;
Perchance our lives, should men be scarce,
  To fight his cause for pay.
We are his slaves ! he owns our lands,
  Our woods, our seas, and skies ;
He'd have us shot like vicious dogs,
  Should we in murm'ring rise !
     Chapeau bas !
     Chapeau bas
  Gloire au Marquis de Carabas !

II.—MY LORD TOMNODDY.

My Lord Tomnoddy's the son of an Earl,
His hair is straight, but his whiskers curl ;
His Lordship's forehead is far from wide,
But there's plenty of room for the brains inside.
He writes his name with indifferent ease,
He's rather uncertain about the ' d's,'—
But what does it matter, if three or one,
To the Earl of Fitzdotterel's eldest son ?

My Lord Tomnoddy to college went,
Much time he lost, much money he spent ;
Rules, and windows, and heads, he broke—
Authorities wink'd—young men will joke !

He never peep'd inside of a book—
In two years' time a degree he took ;
And the newspapers vaunted the honours won
By the Earl of Fitzdotterel's eldest son.

My Lord Tomnoddy came out in the world,
Waists were tighten'd, and ringlets curl'd.
Virgins languish'd, and matrons smil'd—
'Tis true, his Lordship is rather wild ;
In very queer places he spends his life ;
There's talk of some children, by nobody's wife—
But we mustn't look close into what is done
By the Earl of Fitzdotterel's eldest son.

My Lord Tomnoddy must settle down—
There's a vacant seat in the family town !
('Tis time he should sow his eccentric oats)—
He hasn't the wit to apply for votes :
He cannot e'en learn his election speech,
Three phrases he speaks—a mistake in each !
And then breaks down—but the borough is won
For the Earl of Fitzdotterel's eldest son.

My Lord Tomnoddy prefers the Guards,
(The House is a bore) so!—it's on the cards!
My Lord's a Lieutenant at twenty-three,
A Captain at twenty-six is he—
He never drew sword, except on drill ;
The tricks of parade he has learnt but il!—
A full-blown Colonel at thirty-one
Is the Earl of Fitzdotterel's eldest son !

My Lord Tomnoddy is thirty-four ;
The Earl can last but a few years more.
My Lord in the Peers will take his place :
Her Majesty's councils his words will grace.
Office he'll hold, and patronage sway ;
Fortunes and lives he will vote away—
And what are his qualifications?—ONE !
He's the Earl of Fitzdotterel's eldest son.

III.—THE EARL OF WHITECHOKERLEA.

Yon sober carriage of drab you see,
  Whose lamps so biliously glimmer,
Belongs to the Earl of Whitechokerlea,
  The late Lord Felix Trimmer.

'Tis a man to pity, and not to hate ;
He would be good if he durst be great ;
A difficult task he has planned to do—
God he would serve and Mammon too.
He feeds the hind, and instructs the churl,
That Heaven may pardon his being an earl ;
And hopes, by pray'rs both early and late,
The crest on his Bible to expiate,
  And the 'scutcheon, in church, o'er his pew we see,
    Bright gules and golden shimmer—
  The arms of the Earls of Whitechokerlea,
    Whose family name is Trimmer.

To feed six days on the very best,
He'll touch no food on the Sabbath dress'd.

That his name may long in the land remain,
On his lawns he'll have no sports profane.

Penance he does, for receiving rent,
By returning—as much he can—per cent.

His servants, livery wear, 'tis true,
But of sober cut and demurest hue ;

No narrower strip of lace could be,
Than round each footman's 'brimmer,'
In the house of the Earl of Whitechokerlea,
The late Lord Felix Trimmer.

He goes to Court ; but, to make it right,
He'll howl with Stiggins in barns at night.
He votes in the House on the Tory side ;
True to his order, he 'stems the tide ;'
But churches he founds, and the men who preach
Sackcloth and ashes, he orders to teach ;
To live in his castle with conscience squared,
His labourers' hovels he keeps repaired.

That his sons at College may tutor'd be,
His serfs, with horn and primer

Are supplied by the Earl of Whitechokerlea,
The late Lord Felix Trimmer.

His carriage he'll stop, to a famishing group
To give a ticket for flannel and soup ;
A poacher he'll punish according to act,
But send him in prison a meal and a tract ;
He'll fast and pray o'er the labourer's case,
To make him contented, and—stop in his place.
When press'd too hard with the claims of home,
Over the sea will his sympathies roam :
In the Friendly Isles or the Caribbee,
Where the Christian light burns dimmer,
Is a field for the Earl of Whitechokerlea,
The late Lord Felix Trimmer.

Much good he does, but he might do more ;
A life so spent we must all deplore.
Vainly he strives, for conscience's sake,
The best of this world and the next to make.
Would he could make his salvation sure,
By giving up *some* of his goods to the poor—

Say twenty per cent.—on the Judgment Day !

The chapter of Demas, who 'turn'd away,'

    When he reads his Bible, must surely be

        Than ghost or goblin grimmer,

    To the pious Earl of Whitechokerlea,

        The late Lord Felix Trimmer !

IV.—LORD CHARLES CLEVERLEY.

Lord Charles is the hope of the Peerage ;
No fears of a wreck need o'erwhelm
The passengers down in the steerage,
With men like Lord Charles at the helm.
A publisher's shop full of blue books
Is this budding senator's head ;
He has also written a few books,
Much noticed, and some of them read.

He's travell'd o'er Europe and Asia,
Half track'd to its sources the Nile.
(His work, " From Park Lane to Dalmatia,"
Was brought out in wonderful style.)

He's finished five books of a poem,
    And acts of a tragedy four,
Which fortunate people who know him,
    Say, Shakspeare, will certainly floor.

But still from his station's high duties
    His Lordship is not to be won :—
Himself, e'en from Poesy's beauties,
    He tears, when there's work to be done.
He won't let the State (how paternal !)
    Through indolence fall in the lurch.
He edits a talented journal,
    Dissenters to bring back to Church.

To him legislation's a pleasure ;
    (Though by it so many are bored !)
Last session he brought in a measure
    To have the old Maypoles restored ;
And, then, with the people so kindly
    He mixes—their meetings attends—
Advises them not to rush blindly
    In face of their masters and friends !—

His charity, too, so disarming
    To malice—he's founded some schools,
(The costume and badge are most charming!)
    Himself, he has framed all the rules.
With scriptural texts (*his* selecting)
    The walls round are tastily hung:
Content and submission directing,
    As virtues most fit for the young.

At soirées of all institutions,
    As chairman, to act he'll engage;
Of knottiest points, the solutions
    He'll give to men three times his age.
He'll talk agriculture to graziers,
    And bid them to cultivate—grass;
And pats on the head even glaziers,
    And tells them their business is—glass!

'Tis cheering and really delightful
    To see such a promising gem—
A Lord—of Democracy frightful,
    The tide, who has talent to stem

The Peers, they say, care but for plenty,

And won't even work for their pelf!

Here's one who has scarce turned twenty,

Will manage the nation himself!

V.—SIR MENENIUS AGRIPPA, THE FRIEND OF THE PEOPLE.*

1st Citizen. Soft: who comes here?
2nd Cit. Worthy Menenius Agrippa; one that hath always
    loved the people.
1st Cit. He's one honest enough; would all the rest were so.
Men. What work's my countrymen in hand? Where go you
With bats and clubs? The matter? Speak, I pray you.
1st Cit. Our business is not unknown to the senate; they have
had inkling this fortnight what we intend to do, which now we'll
show 'em in deeds. They say poor suitors have strong breaths;
they shall know we have strong arms too.'
Men. Why, masters, my good friends, mine honest neighbours, Will you undo yourselves?
1st Cit. We cannot, sir; we are undone already.
Men. I tell you, friends, most charitable care
Have the patricians of you—

                                    Coriolanus, Act 1, *Scene* 1.

SIR MENENIUS AGRIPPA'S a Radical stout,

With a rental of sixty-five thousand about,

Of opinions the lowest though lofty in grade,

A Sir Walter Fitz-Tyler, a Lord John de Cade.

* This study is little more than a rhymed generalisation of Mr
Whitty's admirable portrait of an individual pseudo radical
baronet in the *Governing Classes.*

You may call him a Leveller—Do, 'tis his pride ;
Nay, a stark staring Democrat—True ! of the tide
He's a wave ; you may stem him, my Lord, if you
 can ;
Sir Menenius Agrippa's a popular man !
 Reform ! Vote by ballot ! Short Parliaments—
 cry !
 Down—down, with each bishop, church, pulpit,
 and steeple !
 The Peerage ? Um ! Ha ! Well, we'll see by
 and bye ?
 Sir Menenius Agrippa's the friend of the people.

He sits for a borough remote from his home,
(Where he reigns like a slave-girt Patrician of
 Rome).
He goes on the hustings in very old coats—
(He's a change at the club) when soliciting votes,
His beard he neglects, and his nails he begrimes,
(His jokes on clean collars are killing at times) ;
Hang your wine ? give him *beer* from the pewter or
 can ;
Sir Menenius Agrippa's a popular man !

Reform ! Vote by ballot ! Short Parliaments—
cry !
Down—down, with each bishop, church, pulpit,
and steeple !
The Peerage ?—Um ! Ha ! Well, we'll see by
and bye !
Sir Menenius Agrippa's the friend of the people.

He hates all routine—lift the cart from the mud !
But the drivers are failing—new blood, sir ! new
blood !
Though the Lords have such pow'r—mind in prin-
ciple quite
Constitutional—oh, most undoubtedly right !
But the men ! an exclusive and arrogant class—
All behind in ideas—not a throb with the mass !
If we *could* to their ranks—Well ! we'll do what we
can—
Sir Menenius Agrippa's a popular man !
Reform ! Vote by ballot ! Short Parliaments—
cry !
Down—down, with each bishop, church, pulpit,
and steeple !

The Peerage?—Um! Ha! Well, we'll see by
and bye!

Sir Menenius Agrippa's the friend of the people.

'Tis said Sir Menenius will soon be a peer,
(He annoyed the Queen's government sadly last
year);
They've a service of plate for him—tarrying but
To make sure if plain "Sir" or "His Lordship" to
cut.
His constituents hiccup, "Oh! just wait a bit
Till *we're* rais'd to the peerage—then see how things
fit—
I oppress us much longer the Oligarch can!"
Sir Menenius Agrippa's a popular man.

Reform! Vote by ballot! Short Parliaments—
cry!

Down—down, with each bishop, church, pulpit,
and steeple!

The Peerage? Um! Ha! Well, we'll see by and
bye!

Sir Menenius Agrippa's the friend of the people.

VI.—SIR GYPES TOLLODDLE, J.P.

AIR—*The Fine Old English Gentleman.*

'TIS said the age is sinking into indolence and
"coddle,"
And that, of ev'ry manly English type, we've lost the
model.
A lay to prove the contrary but now has struck my
noddle,
Descriptive of the virtues of my friend Sir Gypes
Tolloddle.

Who's a fine Old English Gentleman,
Worthy the olden time.

Half Snobshire's his—of Flunkeyshire, he owns at
    least a fourth,
Besides in Wales at Llandevowrdd, a spacious foot of
    earth,
In Ireland too, Kilbeggarman—Clapmammon, in the
    North ;
Sir Gypes thinks highly of himself, yet knows not
    half he's worth—
    As a fine Old English Gentleman,
        Worthy the olden time.

He's sixty-five ; his age, at most, at fifty-four you'd
    fix ;
He's six feet high,—you'd take your oath Sir Gypes
    was six feet six,
So like a lion's is his tread, you fear a lion's
    tricks,
And, when he's pass'd, feel thankful you've escaped
    from blows or kicks,
    From this fine Old English Gentleman,
        Worthy the olden time.

He dresses like a farming man, in russet gray or
  brown,
He carries bundles, cracks his jest with common folk
  "down town,"
" No pride, you see ! like one of us !" but, freedom
  to keep down,
Lurks more than bowstring terror in the true Al
  Raschid frown,
  Of this fine Old English Gentleman,
    Worthy the olden time.

At Quarter Sessions sits Sir Gypes, a judge as Minos
  grim,
A poacher upon his estates, he'd sunder limb from
  limb ;
Sir Gypes is not a cruel man, but has a notion
  dim,
Long taught him, that the greatest crime's a liberty
  with *him*.
  Like a fine Old English Gentleman,
    Worthy the olden time.

He's not a sage ; but ears, to catch his sayings, so
    incline,

The dullest phrase, he speaks as from an oracle
    divine,

You somehow feel quite grateful when he says ' the
    day is fine,'

For placing it past question that the sun *does really*
    shine,

    Like a fine Old English Gentleman,

        Worthy the olden time.

A hat two seconds on a head, he scarcely ever
    saw ;

The earliest word he learnt to speak was register'd as
    law ;

Were you and I to laugh at him, he'd look on us with
    awe

As lunatics escap'd from dungeon, whipping-post, and
    straw,

    Would this fine Old English Gentleman,

        Worthy the olden time.

His butler is a gentleman with thousands in the
bank,

His housekeeper, a lady, ne'er to mix with tradesfolk
sank.

Sir Gypes, of some ten thousand souls, enjoys the
foremost rank

As Number One—the others making up the ciphers
blank,

    To this fine Old English Gentleman,
       Worthy the olden time.

"But is it not," I hear you ask, "a goodly sight to
view?

And would you to the earth a tree, such fruit that
gives us, hew?

Is he not hospitable, brave—above the grov'lling
crew

In stainless honour as in rank—?" I frankly answer
—True!

    He's a fine Old English Gentleman,
       Worthy the olden time.

He's loyal, generous—his word's his bond, to king or
    clown.

I grant him type of all those gifts—have won our
    land renown;

And yet 'tis hard!—six parishes, twelve hamlets,
    and a town,

This splendid sample to produce, should be, as
    'twere, boil'd down,

Of a fine Old English Gentleman,
    Worthy the olden time.

HISTORIC FANCIES.

THE RETURN FROM SYRIA.

Air—*Le départ pour la Syrie.*

It was Dunois, the young and brave, returning
from the wars,
In glory, over head and ears, but wholly free from
scars :
He sung a variation of his old conceited air—
" I've prov'd the bravest brave, and mean to wed
the fairest fair ! "
" Now that's a lie ! " a voice exclaim'd. The
Warrior turn'd him round,
But seeing but a Palmer gray, contemptuously he
frown'd.

"I speak not of the fairest fair," went on the
    Pilgrim knave,
"But I'll be damn'd eternally if thou'rt the
    bravest brave!"

"Thou wear'st a gown!" said young Dunois.   The
    Palmer answer'd, "Pooh!
Come walk your horse up hill ; you've time to hear a
    truth or two,
(You'll hear but few in yonder town).   Say—by
    what doings rare
You've earn'd—(there's ne'er a doubt you'll get)
    the fairest of the fair ?"

Superbly smil'd the young Dunois :—"The trouba-
    dours have told,
Methinks—"   "The troubadours be damn'd!"
    struck in the Vagrant bold,
"At Prince's board, in Baron's tent, they glean
    their news, 'tis known ;
My fancy pictures their accounts—I want to hear
    your own."

" *Ventre St. Gris!* " cried young Dunois, piqu'd
    into language plain ;
" A man, who all the hardships of last winter's
    fierce campaign
Has known, is surely somebody." Replied the Pal-
    mer—" True !
How many of those hardships, pray, were undergone
    by you ? "

" All." " That's a lie !—(nay, be not wroth—you
    know I wear a gown)
Pray name them ? " " Well, the cold—" "Your
    cloak was lined with sable down :
Your lady mother sent out furs to warm you while
    you slept :
To forage fuel for your tent, two freezing hinds
    were kept.

Another instance, pray." " While sick with fever,
    I went out,
And seized the Soldan's standard from a fortified
    redoubt "—

" The wretch who struck its guardian dead, ex-
     hausted by the blow,
Fell dying, killed by soleless boots, and porridge
     diet low.—

Go on ! " Again supremely smil'd Dunois : "A
     night attack,
I recollect, on Joppa, with some hundreds at my
     back,
Of men-at-arms, 'gainst fearful odds ; and hist'ry
     has not spurn'd
The fact, that 'twas their Leader who alone un-
     scathed returned."

" I recollect it too," the Pilgrim's brow grew dark
     and grim—-
" Those men-at-arms wore tatter'd vests, with
     naked head and limb ;
The Leader who return'd unscath'd was clad, from
     head to heel,
In spear and dart-proof armour, of the hardest
     Milan steel."

The sound of bells came on the air, the city bore
in sight—

" Dost hear them, Cynic ? " joyously exclaim'd the
radiant Knight—

"My welcome 'tis !—come, quit thy snarls—our
merry-makings share,

I go to reign the bravest brave, to wed the fairest
fair ! "

The Pilgrim sigh'd, " I journey for an unshriv'd
brother's soul,

Who fell unknown on Joppa's plains ; for him, no
belfries toll.

Farewell, Sir Knight, in Mary's name, your race's
birthright share—

Be held the bravest of the brave—enjoy the fairest
fair ! "

THE INCAS OF PERU.

AIR—*When this old hat was new.*

THERE's no excuse for ignorance, now Baronets
and Earls
Have taken, from the lecture-room, to pelting us
with pearls.
A grateful pig, I've humbly scrap'd to pick up one
or two,
And learnt a few statistics of the Incas of Peru.

No doubt a many in this room may glean a
hint or two,
From what I've just been reading of the Incas
of Peru.
Peru is in America—(you see how I've got on !)
Producing gold in hundredweights, and silver by
the ton ;

With burning plains, but grassy dells, where
cooling breezes lurk ;
The place in fact to live—with some one else to do
the work.

No doubt a many in this room, the self-same
point of view
Would take of it, precisely, as the Incas of
Peru.

The Incas were a Royal Race, descended from the
Sun,
In person quite distinguish'd from the folks of
common run :
They'd smaller hands, and cleaner teeth, a finer
type of nose ;
They had no chilblains on their heels, or corns upon
their toes.

No doubt a many in this room, with marks of
birth in view
Like those, would kiss the shoe-strings of the
Incas of Peru.

In right of their divine descent, they own'd Peru-
    via's soil ;
Of course, such dainty finger-tips were never made
    to toil—
In fact, 'twas 'gainst the laws they should—except
    to bring in pails
Of water, for the monarch's bath, or cut the royal
    nails.
    No doubt a many in this room would swagger
      if they knew
    Gold-Shaving-Pot-in-Waiting, to the Incas of
      Peru.

Now, something like a ruling class were they :
    beneath their rule,
No common person's children were allow'd to go to
    school ;
And none, to hold an office or command, could e'er
    expect—
Save those of Inca families, which kept the thing
    select.

No doubt a many in this room know younger
 sons who rue
Not having such connections as the Incas of
 Peru.

Their priests the people taught, the greatest crime
 was shirking toil ;
And, next to that, begrudging to their lieges all its
 spoil.
The cottar as he delved the mine, or reap'd the
 golden maize,
Was made to sing war songs, in his indulgent
 master's praise.
No doubt a many in this room had earn'd a
 pound or two,
By writing flunkey ballads for the Incas of
 Peru.

The Incas had their game preserves—vast flocks
 of llama goats,
That fatten'd on the workman's corn, like pheasants
 on our oats.

An annual bunch (say one per cent) of fleece each
    serf might pull
At shearing time, 'mid dance and song—much cry
    and little wool !
    No doubt a many in this room will this con-
    cession view,
    As rather feeble-minded in the Incas of Peru !

They'd Poor Laws too, well organis'd—a man his
    work who'd done,
(That is, the Incas') might not to his own poor
    garden run,
Until his neighbours, old and sick, he'd help'd with
    might and main ;
Which sav'd relieving officers—from vagrants
    clear'd the plain.
    No doubt a many in this room, a scandal think
    it, to
    Abuse paternal rulers, like the Incas of Peru.

The people were contented then, like hounds or
    rabbits tame ;

But, well-a-day! one morning fine, Pizarro's cut-
throats came :—

" Peruvians arm!" the Incas cry, "Your plains
and cities fair,

Invaders threaten!" but the people didn't seem to
care.

No doubt a many in this room, as dastard
traitors, view

The hinds, who wouldn't rally round the Incas
of Peru.

The Spaniards cut the Incas' throats; the people
calm look'd on ;

Slaves like a change of masters—they submitted
to the Don ;

He paid as well, allow'd them drink : four cent'ries
have gone round,

The Indians of Peru are still the slaves the
Spaniards found.

No doubt a many in this room, in this recital
true,

Can weep but for the downfall of the Incas of
Peru.

THE APOLOGUE OF CORIOLANUS.

AIR—*Billy Taylor.*

ROMAN history is edifying,
  And though by Niebuhr, in the German
    tongue,
Proved to consist of nine-tenths lying,
  Morals, here and there, may be from it wrung.

Coriolanus was a noble Roman,
  Of ancient birth and lineage high,
Son of a most superior woman,
  One of a ruling fami-ly.

  Roman history is edifying,
    And though by Niebuhr, in the German
      tongue,
  Proved to consist of nine-tenths lying,
    Morals, here and there, may be from it wrung.

When he came to his first moustaches,
    He, by his birthright, with the rest
Took his seat on the Senate's benches
    Learning to govern, spout, and jest.

    Roman history is edifying,
        And though by Niebuhr, in the German
            tongue,
    Proved to consist of nine-tenths lying
        Morals, here and there, may be from it
    wrung.

He got on (for the boy was clever);
    Showing a turn for Diploma-cy,
Off they sent him, a row to settle,
    Pending with the Volsci-i.

    Roman history is edifying,
        And though by Niebuhr, in the German
            tongue,
    Proved to consist of nine-tenths lying,
        Morals, here and there, may be from it
    wrung.

Soon, of Rome, he made the name to

Act as a terror and a spell,

(Titus Jones or Licinius Tomkins,

This, by the way, might have done as well).

Roman history is edifying,

And though by Niebuhr, in the German

tongue,

Proved to consist of nine-tenths lying,

Morals, here and there, may be from it

wrung.

When the Romans came to hear of it,

Much they applauded what he had done,

And they cried, "We want a Consul,

He's the party we must fix upon."

Roman history is edifying,

And though by Niebuhr, in the German

tongue,

Proved to consist of nine-tenths lying,

Morals, here and there, may be from it

wrung.

Spoke the Tribunes of the People,
"Coriolanus, why elect?
He belongs to the class Patrician,
To whose sceptres you object."

Roman history is edifying,
And though by Niebuhr, in the German
tongue,
Proved to consist of nine-tenths lying,
Morals, here and there, may be from it
wrung.

Said the People, "He licked the Volscians;
Rome with honours he has enriched—"
"Bread is dear—he supports high prices."
"Into Aufidius, how he pitch'd?"

Roman history is edifying,
And though by Niebuhr, in the German
tongue,
Proved to consist of nine-tenths lying,
Morals, here and there, may be from it
wrung.

" He's the Sovereign Pontiff's cousin—"
" Corioli's hard siege he won."
" *You*, he has stigmatis'd as vermin—"
" Dear old Corry ! how like his fun ! "

Roman history is edifying,
　　And though by Niebuhr, in the German
　　　tongue,
Proved to consist of nine-tenths lying,
　　Morals, here and there, may be from it
　　　wrung.

So they elected him First Consul
　Of the Roman Commonwealth,
(Spite of the Tribunes' dismal croakings),
　Prais'd his acts, and drank his health.

Roman history is edifying,
　　And though by Niebuhr, in the German
　　　tongue,
Proved to consist of nine-tenths lying,
　　Morals, here and there, may be from it
　　　wrung.

" No more Taxes, no more troubles !

Rome is saved," was the tipsy cry,

" Now we have got the man for Consul

Who pitch'd into the Volsci-i ! "

Roman history is edifying,

And though by Niebuhr, in the German

tongue,

Proved to consist of nine-tenths lying,

Morals, here and there, may be from it

wrung.

" Wars mismanaged, Priests o'er pamper'd,

Slavery, sinecures, prices high,

Coriolanus soon will settle,

Just as he did the Volsci-i."

Roman history is edifying,

And though by Niebuhr, in the German

tongue,

Proved to consist of nine-tenths lying,

Morals, here and there, may be from it

wrung.

But when he came to his manifesto,
  " Rome is sold ! " was the alter'd cry ;
" Coriolanus snubs the People,
  Just as he did the Volsci-i."

    Roman history is edifying,
       And though by Niebuhr, in the German
        tongue,
    Proved to consist of nine-tenths lying,
      Morals, here and there, may be from it
      wrung.

Spoke the Tribunes of the People,
  " You were warn'd—it serves you right."
" That be hanged ! " said the wroth plebeians,
  " Here he insults us morn and night."

    Roman history is edifying,
       And though by Niebuhr, in the German
        tongue,
    Proved to consist of nine-tenths lying.
      Morals, here and there, may be from it
      wrung.

"Calls us greasy hounds and rascals—"
"He's a Lord—to his order true."
"Won't hear a word against priestly rapine—"
"What should a Pontiff's kinsman do?"

Roman history is edifying,
> And though by Niebuhr, in the German
> tongue,
Proved to consist of nine-tenths lying,
> Morals, here and there, may be from it
> wrung.

"Taxes are doubled, and armies perish ;
Slavery spreads." "He's your chosen man."
"Yes, but suppose we chose the wrong one?"
"It can't be help'd!" Said the mob, "It can."

Roman history is edifying,
> And though by Niebuhr, in the German
> tongue,
Proved to consist of nine-tenths lying,
> Morals, here and there, may be from it
> wrung.

E

Soon, by the force of wrath and brickbats,

  Urged from Rome, the Consul flees ;

This is the story of Coriolanus—

  You may apply it how you please.

  Roman history is edifying,

    And though by Niebuhr, in the German

    tongue,

  Proved to consist of nine-tenths lying,

    Morals, here and there, may be from it

    wrung.

A WORD FOR NERO.

Lord J.'s a sage —the Viscount P.

A statesman sound—Lord X., a hero ;

Some good in all the great must be,

Suppose we look for it—in Nero.

There is a tale, devoid of proof,

That, for a lark, he set Rome burning,

And fiddled on his palace roof,

While on, the water plugs were turning ;

Play'd *Fake away* to smoke and flash,

That belch'd forth tints for Martin's easel,

Row Polkas to each homesteads' crash,

To ev'ry death—*Pop goes the Weasel !*

Lord J.'s a sage—the Viscount P.,
  A statesman sound—Lord X., a hero
Some good in all the great must be,
  Suppose we look for it—in Nero.

Now I would credit just as lief
  The vulgar malcontent palaver,
Which hints that our Crimean Chief
  Last winter out at Balaklava,
Gay crowds, with music, jellies, soups,
  Regal'd—within his quarter's crush rooms,
While starv'd, and frozen, round him, troops
  Unburied lay, as thick as mushrooms.

Lord J.'s a sage—the Viscount P.,
  A statesman sound—Lord X., a hero ;
Some good in all the great must be,
  Suppose we look for it—in Nero.

The facts are these—(but writers, so
  On great men's acts are prone to lying !)
Rome had been, not misgovern'd—no,
  But overtax'd, there's no denying.

Wars had been lengthy—conquests few,
   The conscript laws were—well, imperious,
The crops had fail'd—Patricians grew
   Each day more wealthy—things looked serious.

   Lord J.'s a sage—the Viscount P.,
      A statesman sound—Lord X., a hero ;
   Some good in all the great must be,
      Suppose we look for it—in Nero.

Some agitators impious, known
   As Christians, too, the mob had nettled,
(Themselves, to feed the tigers thrown,
   Their doctrines still the crowds unsettled) ;
These spurn'd their gods—revil'd their priests,
   Fight, to the nobles threaten'd showing,
Vow'd they were born as men, not beasts—
   Things were, in fact, to BLAZES going !

   Lord J.'s a sage—the Viscount P.,
      A statesman sound—Lord X., a hero ;
   Some good in all the great must be,
      Suppose we look for it—in Nero.

Of burning Rome, I think the myth,
  I've proved to be a poet's figure.
The ruling classes felt forthwith,
  Measures they must adopt of vigour.
"What's to be done? We're lost, an' we
  Calm not the orders low and middle"—
Nero stepped forth :—"Leave that to me.
  I'll calm them." "How?" "I'll play the
    fiddle!"

Lord J.'s a sage—the Viscount P.,
  A statesman sound—Lord X., a hero ;
Some good in all the great must be,
  Suppose we look for it—in Nero.

Next morn, on ev'ry gate and wall,
  'Stead of seditious squibs ill blooded,
A poster thus :—"*Minerva Hall,*
  Lecture and Concert?" Romans studied—
National Song and Minstrelsy,
  Enlarg'd, in chapter and in verse, on.
Full Band and Chorus! Entrance Free!!
  THE EMP'ROR WILL CONDUCT IN PERSON!!!!"

Lord J.'s a sage—the Viscount P.,

 A statesman sound—Lord X., a hero ;

Some good in all the great must be,

 Suppose we look for it—in Nero.

The hall was throng'd—each air encor'd :

 Delighted by the condescension, :

The mob at each *facetia* roared—

 (Those on the Christians, past all mention !)

They cheered the Emp'ror to his door—

 The nobles all, good, bad, and middling ;

I think I need defend no more

 The moral bent of Nero's fiddling.

Lord J.'s a sage—the Viscount P.,

 A statesman sound—Lord X., a hero ;

There's good in all the great you see—

 I've even found it out—in Nero.

June 12, 1855.

GODIVA.

I.

Godiva! not for countless tomes
    Of war's and kingcraft's leaden hist'ry,
Would I thy charming legend lose
Or view it in the bloodless hues
    Of fabled myth or myst'ry.

II.

Thou tiny pearl of Demagogues!
    Thou blue-eyed rebel—blushing traitor!
Thou *Sans-culotte*, with dimpled toes,
Whose Red cap is an op'ning rose—
    Thou trembling agitator!

III.

We must believe in thee ! Our ranks
　　Of champions loom with faces grimy,—
Fierce Tylers, from the anvil torn,
Rough-chested Tells with palms of horn—
　　Foul Cades, from ditches slimy !

IV.

Knit brows, fierce eyes, and sunken cheeks,
　　Fill up the vista stern and shady ;
Our one bright speck, we cannot spare,
Our reg'ment's sole Vivandière—
　　Our little dainty lady !

V.

No, she was true ! the story old,
　　As any crumbling, Saxon castle,
Firm at its base : she liv'd, and moved,
And breath'd, and all around her, lov'd—
　　Lord, lackey, hound and vassal !

VI.

She lov'd Earl Leofric, her lord,
　　Nor car'd with his fierce moods to wrestle,

By protest more than eyelids red ;
Would he but pat her golden head,
   'Twould in his rude breast nestle.

VII.

She lov'd the palfrey, o'er the plain
   That gallop'd to her voice's chirrup ;
His surly grooms she thought were kind,
Noble and true, she deem'd the hind,
   Who, cringing, held her stirrup.

VIII.

The peacocks on the lawn she lov'd—
   But none the less their homely gray mates.
The kennel yelp'd as near she drew ;
A crippled, ugly cur or two,
   Were her especial playmates.

IX.

She lov'd all things beneath the sun.
   Into the toad's bright eyes, unstartled,
She laughing gazed : within the brake,
She'd wonder—"had she hurt the snake,
   That out upon her dartled?"

X.

Into the peasant's tree-built hut,

    With reeking walls and greasy tables,

She lov'd to run for draughts of milk—

The children maul'd her robe of silk,

    And pull'd to bits her sables.

XI.

They made her sad! she loved them all—

    Each lout, a friend—each drab, a sister—

Why praise her beauty—goodness, so?

Why, when she left them, how so low?

    None of them ever kiss'd her!

XII.

Within the town, 'twas worse than all,

    Where anvil clank'd, and furnace rumbled;

There workmen, starved and trampled, met,

Thought, talk'd, and planned—a churlish set,

    Embitter'd—no whit humbled.

XIII.

They rail'd at her—their tyrant's bride,

    When, like a mouse, she peep'd among them

They met her frighten'd smiles with "Go!"
Her bungling proffered love with "No!"
    What had she done to wrong them?

XIV.

For wrong'd they were, she felt it sore—
    Else, whence such faces wan and gloomy?
In smoke, and filth, and discontent,
Why thousands, thus in alleys pent,
    And earth so rich and roomy?

XV.

She could not tell!   But she would give
    Her soul, the people's wrongs to lighten :
Or, if she might not—in their smoke
Would they but let her with them choke,
    Nor off, with rude words frighten!

XVI.

What could she do?   Dark rumours came
    That 'twas the Earl, her lord and master,
Caused all their wrong.   Alas, the day!
She lov'd him, too—what means essay
    The double-fold disaster,

XVII.

To turn aside ?   The moment came —
      The town new tax'd, moan'd fierce and sadly
" How free them from this task ?" said she.
" *Ride naked through the town*," laugh'd he.
      " I will," she answered, "gladly."

XVIII.

And gladly to her bow'r she fled,
      This more than virgin, gaily singing ;
And stripp'd a form, that morn had blush'd
All over, by a rude fly brush'd,
      Her garden-bath o'erwinging !

XIX.

And gladly on her palfrey sprung,
      That quick the echoing stones awakèd.
"They will be freed !" she sang, "and he
Shall know no harm !"—rose-red, went she,
      That she was proud—not naked !

XX.

She gallop'd through the glaring street—
      'Tis true as written gospel holy.

'Tis also true, thank God ! that all
The meanest mean—the smallest small—
 The vilest of the lowly,

XXI.

Kept within doors, with windows barr'd,
 And pray'd for her with tears and fasting,
Nor on the flying vision bright
Gaz'd, (though a glimpse of heav'n that might
 For torments everlasting,

XXII.

Nigh compensate)—save one alone—
 And here, I own, my faith gets weaker :
'Tis said, a rascal, from behind,
A shutter peep'd, and God struck blind
 The soulless, prying sneaker.

XXIII.

I would not have a miracle
 Bring doubt upon my darling's story ;
God does not thus avenge the true,
But leaves their wrongs to me and you,
 To right them in their glory.

XXIV.

Punished the miscreant was, no doubt,
  Indignantly with pump and gutter ;
But he who, of enslav'd mankind,
The martyr pure, could mock—was blind
  Ere he undid the shutter !   .

"WANTED, AN INDIVIDUAL!"

AN ADVERTISEMENT TO A POPULAR AIR.

(Wanted a Governess.)

WANTED a gentleman, booted and spurr'd—
If from the country the rather preferr'd :
From Huntingdon say—no objection at all
To the dialect strong, with a snuffle and drawl.
His duties would be with a party to deal,
Of some gentlemen's families highly genteel ;—
Oh, particularly genteel !

Wanted a gentleman !
A gentleman wanted !

Wanted a gentleman, red in the nose,

Careless of doublet and easy in hose ;

Warts not objected to—(none, by-the-bye,

Save a practis'd ale brewer need care to apply) :

With a head full of brains, and a heart full of zeal,

To astonish some principles highly genteel ;—

    Oh, particularly genteel !

        Wanted a gentleman !

        A gentleman wanted !

Wanted a gentleman—one who can raise

A patriot army in very few days,

And lead them o'er Shams and Delusions roughshod,

For the freedom of England, the glory of God !

Who, by sulphur and flame, dares with hornets to

    deal,

Though their nests be in Abbeys and Castles

    genteel ;—

    Oh, particularly genteel !

        Wanted a gentleman !

        A gentleman wanted !

                F

Wanted a gentleman—ready to plump
On a Long-winded Parliament—kicking it thump
Out of doors, and remain the Right Man in His
  Place.
Having spurn'd as a Bauble the toy call'd a mace—
Ay! and ready in similar language to deal
With Insignia-tomfooleries far more genteel ;—
  Oh, ineffably more genteel!

Wanted a gentleman!
A gentleman wanted!

Wanted a gentleman—one who can make
The tyrants of Europe to shiver and quake,
And can shield, by a word, the poor slaves 'neath
  their rule,
As a master, small boys, from the bullies at school,
While he vulgarly spits on the lackeys who kneel
At his footstool, from sovereigns highly genteel ;—
  Most legitimately genteel !

Wanted a gentleman!
A gentleman wanted!

Wanted a gentleman—write (postage free),

To the People of England, and sign with " O.C."—

Pray don't all speak together!—Not *one* such ?

    Alack !—

There *was* one, but he, some two centuries back,

From a gallows, when dead, was hung up by the heel,

By the founder of three or four houses genteel !—

    Oh, excruciatingly genteel !

        Wanted a—(we really don't know
what to call it) !

        A—(you know the sort of thing we
mean)—wanted !

MISCELLANIES.

"VULGAR DECLAMATION."

A LESSON FOR THE YOUNG.

"But, Sir, I do protest against the language we have heard this evening from the Hon. Member for Aylesbury, who, while he performs what he thinks a public duty in pointing out old errors and instances of mismanagement in regard to the army, must needs tell me that this country has become the laughing-stock of Europe, and has thought proper to mingle with his observations and comments a deal of what I must call vulgar declamation against the aristocracy of this country." (Cheers.)

Lord Palmerston's Speech.

My son, if Fate in store for you

Should have the wond'rous bounty,

To let you live to represent

A borough or a county—

I'd have you do your duty well.

According to your station,

And guard, o'er all, against the use

Of VULGAR DECLAMATION.

I hope you'll never tell the House
    That all men's rights are equal—
That woe to Nations, still must be
    Of Monarchs' Wars the sequel ;
Or that a pauper can be found
    In all the British nation :
For if you do, you'll be accused
    Of VULGAR DECLAMATION.

Avoid allusions to the Church,
    Except, indeed, to praise it ;
Don't rail against a Bishop's pay,
    But give your vote to raise it ;
Don't say that forty-pounds a-year
    Is scant remuneration
For working clergymen, because
    That's VULGAR DECLAMATION.

The Prince of Wales is just your age,
    Together you will grow up ;
He'll soon want money and a wife,
    Don't—when the time comes—blow up

His marriage grant, however great,

Or heavy on the nation—

That stinting princes is the worst

Of VULGAR DECLAMATION.

And then when common soldiers claim

Their share of wealth and glory,

And grudge the lions all the prize,

Don't *you* take up the story.

And as for giving working men

Ideas above their station,

'Tis positively wrong, as well

As VULGAR DECLAMATION.

And, lastly —if some noble name

Should get by chance mix'd up in

Some awkward case of "starved to death,"

Or arsenic, a cup in,

Just hush it up, and hope, at least,

There's some exaggeration ;

But don't, for Heaven's sake, indulge

In VULGAR DECLAMATION.

THE TERRIERS AND THE RATS AND THE MICE AND THE CATS.

A FABLE.

I.

Once on a time—no matter how,
(By force of teeth, or mere " Bow-wow,"
Let studious minds determine)—
The Terriers upon Rat-land, seiz'd,
Its natives hunted, worried, teas'd,
In short—exactly what they pleas'd
Did, with the whisker'd vermin.

II.

They ate them up, when bones ran short;
They chased them to their holes for sport,
They seiz'd their garner'd riches,

(The toothsome cheese—the ripen'd grain);

Monopolised the sunny plain,

Leaving the Rats the loathsome drain—

The gutters, swamps, and ditches.

III.

Coincidence is Hist'ry's joy.

Awhile the Terriers fierce destroy,

Hunt, trample, rob, and feed on

The ever-multiplying Rats,

The Ancient, Warlike race of Cats

Against the Mice, in neighb'ring flats,

Like principles, proceed on.

IV.

And so the Rats and Mice are cow'd,

And so the Cats and Terriers proud,

Live in triumphant clover ;

The Terriers for the Rats make laws,

Cat-Leglisation Mousedom awes ;

Each conquered people—teeth or claws

Held *in terrorem* over !

V.

Spite of the Terriers, throve the Rats ;
Not quite so well, beneath the Cats,
   Got on the pigmy friskers ;
Right jolly dogs the Terriers were,
For bones and pastime, all their care—
(Besides, the Rats would sometimes dare
   To show their teeth and whiskers !)

VI.

So long as Tripe and Lights galore,
Were in the Lordly kennel's store,
   The Rats might live, and welcome ;
Nay—(birds and coneys deft to chase)—
Their Rulers gave them sun and space ;
Only in dearth and famine's case,
   Then would the subject's knell come!

VII.

Not so the Cats—not so the Mice.
Grimalkin's tastes are high and nice,
   And Mousey's views fastidious ;

Cat never likes to leave the house,
O'er plains to run, in streams to souse,
Familiarity with Mouse,
    Were profanation hideous !

VIII.

'Tis Mouse's place to yield him food—
On Mouse's ever-teeming brood,
    'Tis his to feed and fatten.
He by the chimney corner sits,
In velvet coat, and silken "mits,"
Watching his spotless thriving kits,
    Who, but on Mouse-flesh, batten.

IX.

But Mice are small quick-witted wights,
With large round eyes that see great lights :
    To live, and feed, and revel,
They felt their right ; and no wise scared,
(Save prudently), their tyrants dared
To criticise—and schemes prepared
    To send them to the devil.

X.

They met in corners and in holes,
These small conspirators, with souls
    For Truth and Action mighty.
Their themes —Existence, Corn, and Cheese,
On which their purring tyrants seize.
No panic fears their councils freeze,
    No visions wild or flighty

XI.

Their projects mar. Mere Common Sense
Directs their plans—"The Cats must hence,
    And we, about, must bring it.
Many must die, ere ends our wrong;—
Speak, Orators! the weak make strong,
Each singing Mouse who knows a song
    That's warlike—let him sing it."

XII.

The plans were ripe. The dozing Cats,
On velvet chairs and fring-ed mats,
    Began to feel uneasy.

A needle through the cushion pokes ;
A lighted match the whisker smokes ;
('Tis wondrous how the smallest folks,
　Whom you have wrong'd, can tease ye !)

XIII.

And now, a coat of furry silk,
Is dabb'd with pitch ; and now, of milk,
　A saucer rare, is shatter'd.
And now a snow-white paw, that yet
Ne'er damp contamination met,
Steps on a marbled floor, with wet
　And slimy mud, bespatter'd.

XIV.

Up went the lordly backs with rage :
"So, ho ! the pigmies dare to wage
　A war with us !" they mutter'd.
" Quick, measures prompt, we'll make suffice "—
Their claws they sharpen'd in a trice ;
A thousand palpitating Mice
　About their court-yards flutter'd.

XV.

But little Mice have kindreds wide.
For every little mangled hide,
  Of victim, sleek and glossy,
A score of bead-like eyes burnt bright
For vengeance—in the cellar's night,
In workshop's gloom, on gran'ry's height,
  Out in the corn-field mossy.

XVI.

From far and near, the myriads came.
Vengeance and Right, the pigmies claim—
  "Down with the Traps and Poison !"
White gleam the teeth, and red the eye ;
The Tyrant Cats, torn piecemeal, die,
Or panic-stricken, howl and fly,
  Pressed by the madd'ning noise on.

XVII.

The Mice were freed ! The Cats who fled,
With draggled fur, and eyes all red,
  And most with haunches gory--

All blinded by their wild'ring fear,
Plung'd, swimming, o'er the neighb'ring mere,
To Ratland ; and I've kept till here
    The marrow of my story.

XVIII.

The Terriers met them on the shore :
They had been ancient foes before,
    But still the Curs were kindly.
They gave them milk, and fire and food,
Marvelling, in their houndish mood,
How Cats, to rule an insect brood
    Of Mice, could fail so blindly.

XIX.

Answer'd the Cats, " Nay, marvel we,
If little Mice so dauntless be,
    How you the Rats can master––
A fiercer race." The Terriers laugh'd,
" Had you but learnt our plans to graft
On yours, you'd had a certain raft
    To cling to in disaster."

G

XX.

The Cats in chorus mew'd, " Explain,
Oh ! teach us how to pow'r regain,
   And, faith, those Mice shall rue it ! "
The Terriers said, " 'Tis now too late,
You should have earned their love, not hate ;
We our fierce Rats conciliate,
   And this is how we do it :

XXI.

" When game and birds are far from cheap,
And we, a little extra deep,
   Are forced, for private eating,
Into the Rats to dip—and they
Turn rusty, and their tusks display,
(As once they will do, in a way)
   With reeds and spear-grass, meeting,

XXII.

" We beckon out the biggest rat,
And ask him, with a friendly pat,
   To join our side—the merrier—

We teach him how to bark ; with shears,
We dock his tail, and trim his ears,
Give him some bones, to calm his fears,
  And tell him he's a Terrier."

WHO'S AFRAID?

A TAUNT.

So! my lords and gentlemen,
    You are pale!
Sniff ye something hurtful then
    On the gale?
Whence, this toadying the crowd,
Spurn'd, but now, with bearing proud?—
We must "chaff" this aspect cow'd
    New display'd—
(Hitting when you're down's allow'd)
    Who's afraid?

CHORUS (*ad libitum*)

Ya—a—a—a—ah!!!
Who's afraid?

Why, my Lords! you used to case
    All in gold,
Forth in silk, brocade, and lace,
    Bravely stroll'd.
Dress'd like Tom and Dick I vow,
All in black from sole to brow,
Sneakingly, observance, now,
    You evade,
Like a man who dreads a row—
    Who's afraid?

        Chorus (*ad libitum*)

        Ya—a—a—a—ah!!!
        Who's afraid?

Books you're writing, too, I see,
    By the mile,
Not the sort that used to be
    Held the style.
'Stead of Chloe's flow'ry lodge—
"Ventilation"—draining dodge,
Cisterns, pigsties, cheap hodge-podge,

Eggs new-laid !—

Whence this care for Giles and Hodge ?

Who's afraid ?

CHORUS (*ad libitum*)

Ya—a—a—a—ah ! ! !

Who's afraid ?

Then again—we never hear

Of the flights,

Nobles after punch and beer

Took at nights.

In their stead, we've lectures long

By the Peers, on "Art and Song,"—

Pointing all the moral strong—

"Class array'd,

'Gainst its ruling class, is wrong "—

Who's afraid ?

CHORUS (*ad libitum*)

Ya—a—a—a—ah ! ! !

Who's afraid ?

Queer concessions to you make.

From the Church,

Spoils ill-gotten wherefore take—

In the lurch

Leaving Kith and Kin !   To Thought,

Long with burdens over-fraught,

Whence this succour, newly brought,

Long delay'd ?

Surely not "because you ought ?"—

Who's afraid ?

CHORUS (*ad libitum*)

Ya—a—a—a—ah ! ! !

Who's afraid ?

No—my Gentlemen and Lords !

You are sunk

(You'll get used to vulgar words)

In a funk !

Ne'er did wolf, to whom appeal'd

Weeping ewe, a lambkin yield,

Till he saw the shepherd wield

Gun or blade,

In the next-door neighbour's field—

Who's afraid?

CHORUS (*witheringly*)

Ya—a—a—a—ah ! ! ! ! !

Who's afraid ?

" ÇA IRA ! "

A SONG FOR MINISTERS

Imitated from John Oxenford's recently-published Translation.

ALL will go right—will go right—will go right ;
All will succeed, though committees are strong ;
All will go right—will go right—will go right ;
Thus sing the Ministers morning and night.
Meetings may storm, and petitions affright ;
We can afford of such things to make light !
All will go right—will go right—will go right—
  Cracking joke and quoting song,
  We'll hold on to office tight.
All will go right—will go right—will go right—
All will succeed, though committees are strong.

What the *Times* croaks, in the Oligarch's spite,

Means but the "pleb" and the "cad" * to delight;

All will go right—will go right—will go right;

(Now the stamp's off,† they must customers seek !)—

But to suppose that the nation is quite

Ripe for a shindy, and means to show fight,

Putting its heaven-born rulers to flight,

If we don't yield to persuasions polite,

Is of absurdity really the height.

Though the storm blows, 'twill be over ere night;

Send for your brothers—your cousins invite,

    Our's the ship from brow to peak,

    Come on board, no leak's in sight !

All will go right—will go right—will go right—

All will succeed, though committees are strong.

All will go right—will go right—will go right—

Bother the Radical members and prints !

All will go right—will go right—will go right,

Taxes are heavy, let speeches be light :

* Slang terms of contempt, used in the literature of Modern Conservatism to express the classes to which the writers usually belong.

† In allusion to the recent abolition of the stamp on newspapers.

Praise the low rascals who perish in fight;

Give a few sergeants commissions (their plight

Need not be envied !); make some one a knight

Sprung from the ranks; those who still see the light,

Treat with sound coffee and boots water-tight:

Thus aristocracy popular quite

Soon will be render'd, and hailed with delight.

> Pshaw! what nonsense are the hints
>
> That we live on tenure slight!

All will go right—will go right—will go right—

All will succeed, though committees are strong.

All will go right—will go right—will go right,

While the great Palmerston's intellect clear

(All will go right—all will go right—will go right)

Dazzles and floors with its epigrams bright;

Proving that noblemen, only, can fight;

Asking why millers wear hats that are white ?—

When doors are not doors?—What makes us, at night,

All go to bed ?—Where, when went out the light,

Was Moses, the chief of the tribe Israelite ?

(It could not have been in the Commons' house—

> quite).

With such wit, what need we fear
For our privileges' might ?
All will go right—will go right—will go right—
All will succeed, though committees are strong.

All will go right—will go right—will go right,
Papers may bully, and meetings may rave,
Folks in the gutter may starve out of sight,
Fevers may wither, and choleras blight,
War ships may sink, magazines may ignite,
Suicide bankrupts may razors make bright ;
Wine is abundant, and damask is white,
Let us to supper and see out the night—
Put up the shutters to keep out the light
    That already 'gins to brave
    Threat'ningly our blearèd sight.
All will go right—will go right—will go right—
All will succeed, though committees are strong.

THE STRAWBERRY LEAF.

Air—*The Ivy Green.*

Oh, a dainty plant is the strawberry leaf,
  He groweth from ruins old :
Of right choice food he must pick the chief,
  In his cell so lone and cold.
The land must be fertile, and rich the glade,
  To pleasure his dainty whim ;
And triumphs of art, that years have made,
  Must be kept aside for him,
      Eating all, to the nation's grief,
     A hungry plant is the strawberry leaf.

Sure he creepeth on (for he wears no wings,
  But a slow old coach is he) ;

How quickly he findeth, how tightly he clings,
  To good things, wherever they be.
And spreading his tendrils along the ground,
  Each labouring foot he enslaves,
And joyously hugs, as he thrives around,
  The mould of dead warriors' graves.
    Flourishing on, amidst death and grief,
    A poisonous plant is the strawberry leaf.

But a garden fair to be overrun
  With a noxious troublesome weed,
Is a sign of the gardener's work ill done,
  And must remedied be with speed.
So, torn by the roots from each bed and tree,
  And into the bonfire cast,
To blaze on the dunghill, perchance, may be
  The strawberry's fate at last.
    Burnt like straw, in a piled-up sheaf,
    We'll hail the smoke from the strawberry leaf.

"A GENTLEMAN."

Air—*The Island Home of an Englishman.*

There is a word in the English tongue,
  Where I'd rather it were not,
For shams and lies from it have sprung,
  And heartburns fierce and hot.
'Tis a tawdry cloak for a dirty soul—
  'Tis a sanctuary base,
Where the fool and the knave themselves may save
  From justice and disgrace.
    'Tis a curse to the land—deny it who can?
    That self-same boast, "I'm a gentleman!"

It means (if a meaning definite
  Can be fix'd to the thing at all)

A well-cut coat, a faultless boot,
    A hand that's white and small ;
A head well-brush'd, and a shirt well-wash'd,
    A lazy heartless stare ;
Some sterling pounds, *or* a name that sounds
    With the true patrician air.
        These are all you want—deny it who can ?
        To attain the rank of a gentleman !

But with those claims you may take your ease,
    And lounge your long life through,
Without straining a muscle, a nerve, or a thought,
    For the world will work for you.
You may be a dolt, or a brute, or a rogue
    (In a gentlemanly way),
You may drink, you may bet, you may run in debt,
    And never need wish to pay.
        There's an amnesty given—deny it who can ?
        For all the sins of " a gentleman ! "

You may leave your wife, with her children six,
    In a ditch to starve and pine,

And another man's take, in a palace rich,
  With jewels and gold to shine.
You may flog your horse or your dog to death—
  You may shoot it, in a fit of rage,
A helpless groom—and an easy doom
  You'll meet from the jury sage,
    "There's been provocation—deny it who can?
    For we see at a glance he's a gentleman!"

Yet 'tis not for the thousand bulls above
  (Though they trample us and gore),
But the myriad frogs in the marsh below,
  That the evil we deplore.
From spotted wife and tadpoles black,
  The aspiring reptile flies;
He swells too fast, and bursts at last;
  Exclaiming as he dies—
    "A terrible scamp—deny it who can?
    I've been, but I've lived *like a gentleman!*"

FRENCH AND ENGLISH.

A MORALITY FROM THE TRENCHES.

I READ in Friday's *Times*,
  'Midst warlike news affrighting,
Of a soldier blade, who a turn display'd
  Of the highest—for fighting.

A sergeant in the line,
  Of the Thirtieth was he,
Or the Thirty-third (that *or's* a word
  Conveys a deal to me!)

He was left alone to fight
  Five Cossacks fierce and grim ;
One he'd shot—a second had got
  His *quietus* from him.

The three were upon him down,
  He felt as good as dead.
Five cuts he'd had, when he felt the pad
  Of a horse hoof near his head.

The Russians turn'd and fled ;
  He scrambled up as he could,
And was dragg'd by force a-top of the horse
  Like a sack or a log of wood.

Two hundred yards or more,
  O'er outwork, field, and trench,
Their course they wend—when it prov'd his
      friend
  Was a General of the French !

He placed the brave man down
  Safe in the battle's rear—
And (homage grand !) he kiss'd his hand,
  Dropping a rev'rend tear !

Then back to the ranks of Death
  He gallop'd as swift as flame.

And the Sergeant cries—he would give his eyes
    To know that General's name.

I read in the self-same print,
    Ten days ago or more,
Of another blade in the fighting trade,
    Who had faced the cannon's roar.

Had faced the cannon's roar ?
    He had shoved his head in its mouth !
He had strewn the plain with grinning slain ;
    There in the burning South.

He had chopp'd the Russians' limbs,
    Had scatter'd their murky brains,
Had pepper'd them here, and kipper'd them
      there,
    On the hot Crimean plains !

And the fame of his wondrous pluck,
    Throughout the camps they quote.
So Lord Raglan sent for the man to his
      tent,
    And gave him a five-pound note !

In France, the hero's hand
  They kiss with rev'rence dumb.
On English grounds five scurvy pounds,
  Are thought of his worth the sum !

More thoroughly English blood
  Than mine could in no veins dance ;
But matters I own like those I've shown,
  They order much better in France.

A FEW QUESTIONS.

WHY is a cobbler ashamed of his last ?
Why should a tinker stand aghast
    At mention of tongs or kettle ?
Why should the sight of a goose or shears,
Blood, to a tailor's forehead and ears,
    Bring, like the touch of a nettle ?

Why does a barber, a razor spurn ?
Why does a stationer wrathful turn
    When told that he sells lead pencil ?
Why is a shopman annoy'd at "shop ?"
Why does the merchant of door-mat and mop,
Turn from the vendor of heath-broom's crop ?
Why does the kettle hard names let drop
    On the other domestic utensil ?

A FEW MORE.

(IN ANSWER TO THE FOREGOING.

WHY, in the Western Auction Mart,
Do the high-priced slaves strut, knowing and smart,
And in proud contempt, from the contact start,
    Of the "lots" at humble figures?
Why does Adolphe, the mulatto, shrink
From Uncle Tom, with his brow of ink?
Why is it Rosa, with cheeks half-pink,
    At wool-crown'd Topsy, sniggers?
Why, of the chain, should each welded link
    Its fellows abuse as "Niggers?"

FINIS.

www.ingramcontent.com/pod-product-compliance
Lightning Source LLC
Chambersburg PA
CBHW030629270326
41927CB00007B/1362